the world of OLEGAS TRUCHANAS

1 *Death Valley*

the world of OLEGAS TRUCHANAS

Max Angus

First published 1975

© 1975 Melva Truchanas

All rights reserved

ISBN 0 9598212 0 1

Set in Caledonia type
Printed on 157 gsm Enamelet

Electronic scanning of
colour transparencies on
Magnascan 460 by Wilke and
Company Limited at their premises,
37-49 Browns Road, Clayton, Victoria

Designed by Max Angus

Wholly set up, printed and bound
in Australia by Wilke and Company Limited,
37-49 Browns Road, Clayton, Victoria

 First published by the OLEGAS TRUCHANAS PUBLICATION COMMITTEE Hobart

(P.O. Box No. 1 Sandy Bay Tas. 7005)

OLEGAS TRUCHANAS PUBLICATION COMMITTEE

Max Angus	(President)	Frank Bolt
Patricia Giles	(Secretary)*	Peter Dombrovskis
Elspeth Vaughan	(Treasurer)	Ralph Hope-Johnstone
Ray Barnes		Norman Laird

PRODUCTION:

Colour and monochrome photographic selection:
Ralph Hope-Johnstone, Peter Dombrovskis, Ray Barnes, Frank Bolt

Preparation of preliminary colour and monochrome prints:
Ralph Hope-Johnstone

Colour-proofing supervision: Peter Dombrovskis

Art Editor	Max Angus
Editor	Norman Laird

Fourth edition published by O.B.M. Publishing, 96 Collins St. Hobart

* Brenda Hean, Secretary to the committee during its first months, lost her life on a
flight between Hobart and Canberra in September 1972, when the light aircraft in
which she travelled with pilot Max Price vanished without trace.
The purpose of this flight was to perform sky writing over Parliament House in
Canberra as a protest against the proposed flooding of Lake Pedder.

Distributed by O.B.M. PTY. LTD. 96 Collins St. Hobart.

Contents

(Unless otherwise acknowledged, all photographs in this volume are by Olegas Truchanas)

EDITOR'S PREFACE

For beauty is the most unforgettable thing in the world, and
though of it a few perish, and the myriads die unknowing and
uncaring, beneath it the nations of men move as beneath their
pilgrim star. Therefore he who adds to the beauty
of the world is of the sons of God.

FIONA MACLEOD *in*
Deirdre and the Sons of Usna

OLEGAS TRUCHANAS, THE SUBJECT of Max Angus' eloquent memoir, added a new dimension to our knowledge of Tasmania. With his camera he captured an enchanting beauty that had been seen by few people. He did add to the beauty of the world by his presence when alive. Now that he is gone, there is no doubt that he will continue to do so through this classic volume, which was assembled by his friends and published through the generosity of many conservation-minded people and organizations throughout the nation. This opportunity is taken to thank them for their faith and support of the project.

It was the hope of the explorer that one day he might find time to produce a book showing many of the works reproduced here, together with an outline of his views on conservation. His death prevented this. It was the thought of the possible waste of his efforts and talents that moved the author, Max Angus, on the sad day of the funeral of Olegas Truchanas, to propose to close friends of the explorer, the publication of a memorial volume of his activities and photographs.

These friends, nine in number, voluntarily and freely accepted tasks over a period of nearly three years, to enable this work to be completed. It was a happy chance that they were professionals with long backgrounds in one or more of the arts. All share a love of nature, and in particular the wild landscapes of Tasmania. This fortunate combination of likes and skills is reflected in the care and thought lavished on the production, which has the added distinction of being set up and printed in Australia by Australian craftsmen, who from the outset viewed the production as a prestigious one.

Together with thirty other plates of like quality, this book presents fourteen superb photographs of Lake Pedder by the explorer, who with half the nation, found the destruction of this heritage a folly hard to understand. The uncritical fiat which spelled its death arose from the mystique of economic development at any cost. Looking back on the tragedy, one is inclined to agree with J. K. Galbraith's satirical comment that the wiping out of an environment is not so much a failure of the economic system as an integral part of it.

For some people, the environment of the wilderness is no more than a commodity to be used. For them, there is no beauty that cannot be made more beautiful by the menace of 'improvement'. The decrees springing from the illusions of their pragmatic breed have all too often brought disaster to Tasmania's scenery and wild-life. It is to be sincerely hoped that the majestic South-West is not a *silent* target in the dreams of the exploiters.

Olegas Truchanas implied many times that enthusiasm and deep conviction are necessary if men are to explore the alternative possibilities in the emergent conservation ethic. He believed that such conviction must go armed with speculative liberty and unsparing criticism. Of the dangers ahead, he cautioned his friends not to dwell so much on causes as upon circumstances. For it is in the chain of conditions that are to be found the reasons for hidebound resistance to conservation.

Natural wilderness once destroyed is impossible to recreate—a fact hardly considered by those with territorial and economic ambitions. The *rapprochement* between human aims and nature in Tasmania has recently made some progress, but the picture must remain dismal while the law-makers can be depended upon to repeat the mistakes and stratagems of their ancestors. Without doubt, protective attitudes to our existing wilderness need to be intensified, and fortified by concentrated studies likely to influence wide opinion. In those senses, this work is a most valuable addition to the literature of conservation, exploration and the art of photography.

Norman Laird

LEIDĖJO ĮŽANGA

Nes grožis yra labiausiai neužmirštamas dalykas pasaulyje; ir nors
kai kas nuo jo žūsta, nors tūkstančiai ir milijonai miršta
nežinodami ir nesirūpindami, tačiau vedama to grožio,
lyg likimo žvaigždės, žmonija žengia pirmyn. Todėl, kas
plečia pasaulio grožį, yra vienas iš Dievo sūnų.

FIONA MACLEOD *in*

Deirdre and the Sons of Usna

OLEGAS TRUCHANAS, APIE KURĮ KALBA Max Angus savo turiningame prisiminime, praturtino mūsų žinias apie Tasmaniją. Su savo foto aparatu jis atskleidė užburtą grožybę, kurią tik nedaugelis matė. Gyvendamas mūsų tarpe, Olegas Truchanas prisidėjo prie padidinimo pasaulio grožio. Dabar, kai jo jau nebėra, tą darbą tęs be abejo ši nemirštanti knyga. Ją sudarė Olego draugai, o dosnumas daugelio gamtos mylėtojų bei organizacijų palengvino ją išleisti. Ta proga dėkojame visiems už tikėjimą į šį darbą ir už paramą.

Keliautojas-tyrinėtojas Olegas Truchanas vylėsi, kad vieną dieną jis suras laiko surinkti savo fotografijas ir išleisti knygą, tokią, kaip ši, kartu pridėdamas savo mintis ir pažiūras apie gamtos užlaikymą. Jo mirtis tą sutrukdė. Liko tik mintis, kad jo pastangos ir sugebėjimai nenueitų niekais. Ir tą liūdną laidotuvių dieną Max Angus pasiūlė artimiesiems velionio draugams išleisti knygą apie Olego darbus ir veiklą.

Draugai, kurių buvo devyni, savanoriškai pasidalino pareigomis ir dirbo beveik trejus metus, kol pagaliau veikalą užbaigė. Laimingu sutapimu visi devyni buvo gerai patyrę tai vienoj tai kitoj šio darbo srityje. Visi vienodai mylėjo gamtą, o ypatingai neapgyventus Tasmanijos plotus. Tą patirtį ir meilę jie gausiai išliejo į šį rūpestingai paruoštą kūrinį, kuris pasižymi dar ir tuo, kad jį surinko ir spausdino Australijoje, Australijos amatininkai, nuo pat pradžios matę, kad veikalas bus iškilus ir vertingas.

Šalia trisdešimties rinktinių tyrinėtojo fotografijų šioje knygoje dar randame keturiolika puikiausių Pedder ežero nuotraukų. Velionis, kaip ir pusė visos Australijos, negalėjo suprasti tos beprotybės, kurios pasėkoje buvo sunaikinta tokia gamtos dovana. Neapgalvotas veiksmas, kuris reiškė mirtį grožybei, buvo lyg koks užkeikimas – plėstis, tik plėstis, nesvarbu kokia kaina. Žvelgiant atgal į šią tragediją, kyla mintis, kad, nors su pašaipa, J. K. Galbraith teisingai sakė, jog visiškas gamtos nuniokojimas yra ne tiek ekonominės sistemos nepasisekimas, kiek neišvengiamybė.

Yra žmonių, kuriems nesudrumsta aplinka yra vien žaliava išnaudojimui. Jiems nėra tokio grožio, kurio negalima būtų dar kaip nors pagražinti ar "pataisyti". Ir kaip dažnai šios savanaudžių veislės vaizduotėje gimę potvarkiai nešė pražūtį Tasmanijos gamtai ir gyvūnijai! Tikėkime, kad didingieji Tasmanijos Pietvakariai nebus tyli kėslingų išnaudotojų auka.

Olegas Truchanas dažnai sakydavo, kad reikia užsidegimo ir gilaus įsitikinimo, jei žmonės ieško būdų, kaip gamtą apsaugoti. Jis tikėjo, kad reikia išbandyti visus kelius ir priemones ir nenusileisti, sutikus kliūtis. Jis perspėjo savo draugus, kad negaištų ieškodami priežasčių, nes atrastų tik pasiteisinimus dėl atkaklaus pasipriešinimo gamtos užlaikymui.

Sunaikinus žmogaus nepaliestą aplinką, jau jos nebeatkursi — tai tiesa, apie kurią mažai pagalvoja siekią grobio ir pelno. Pastaruoju metu Tasmanijoje santaika tarp žmogaus tikslų ir gamtos pasistūmėjo pirmyn. Tačiau ateities vaizdas tebelieka niūrus ir miglotas, jei pagalvojame, kad įstatymų leidėjai gali vėl pakartoti tas pačias klaidas, tas pačias užmačias, kaip ir jų pirmtakūnai. Tad be abejonės reikia ugdyti gamtos meilę, stiprinti jos užlaikymo reikalą sutelktais mokslo darbais, kurie paveiktų viešąją nuomonę. Ta prasme šis veikalas yra ypač vertingas įnašas į gamtos apsaugojimo bei tyrinėjimo literatūrą, o drauge ir įnašas į fotografijos meną.

Norman Laird

Lithuanian translation by Aleksandras Kantvilas, Hobart

List of colour plates

(Colour plate on back of book jacket by Trevor Spargo)

The salon monochromes*

Illustrations

Olegas Truchanas

a memoir by Max Angus

ILLUS. 1

1

A MAN WHO ACHIEVES EMINENCE in any field stands apart from his fellows. If that field involves the singlehanded exploration of wilderness, with journeys of the most arduous and exceptional kind, he is likely to be set farther apart. A certain air of mystery attaches to him. He is seen to be a solitary man—a loner. Olegas Truchanas was such a man.

At no time could "loner" have seemed more apt than in February of 1958, as Truchanas approached Strahan, a tiny seaport on the west coast of Tasmania. He drifted along in a canvas-covered kayak. He used no paddle. Instead, he had made, from sticks, a jury-mast, and rigged it with a ground-sheet for a sail. A length of cord secured the sail to the big toe of his right foot, to enable him to steer the craft according to wind-shifts, and to leave his hands free to hold the book he was reading.

He was sailing on Macquarie Harbour, a sheet of water more than one hundred square miles in area. Strahan, near its mouth, is its only port. There is neither road to, nor habitation on any other part of its shores. Yet this strange craft had appeared, like a ghost and from the wrong direction . . . east. (The only outlet from Strahan to the open sea is west.) Seeing it, three baffled men leapt into a motor launch and set off towards the tiny craft, now moving closer. The launch throttled down. The man in the kayak continued reading, without glance or sign that he had even noticed the sleek craft that left the curving wake, now closing to full circle around him. No-one spoke. Not a single word was directed to the man with the lowered eyes and brooding expression. So unbelievable and unexpected the encounter, they might have been watching a film, and they watched with the silence of film-goers. Finally they looked away with the embarrassment of the totally ignored and set off for home.

The kayak drew closer to the little harbour then swung neatly in to the old wharf and was made secure. A few children gathered and asked the man where he had come from. "Lake Pedder," he said with a smile. The children looked blank, except the eldest who realised that this stranger must have come down the Gordon River. But the Gordon estuary was over twenty miles away at the eastern end of Macquarie Harbour. He knew that no-one had ever come down the Gordon. Only local men went up—not far at that. There were rain forests, terrifying gorges narrow as slits, rapids, rocks, whirlpools. Some said the river ran underground in places. A sudden storm could raise the river level by more than a hundred feet up the walls of these gorges. No-one lived there, yet someone had told him that this river carried more water than any other in Australia.

Followed by wondering looks from the children, the stranger walked across the road to the post office. He telephoned his wife, Melva, in Hobart, and said, "I am here."[1] Olegas Truchanas, post-war migrant had navigated the Serpentine and Lower Gordon rivers alone—a feat never before accomplished in all the years of European settlement. It remains an epic. A few weeks later he presented a collection of colour slides of his Gordon River voyage to an audience that overflowed the Hobart Town Hall.

He arrived in Tasmania in 1948. Now, ten years later, his name was known to conservationists, bush-walkers, photographers, canoeists, yachtsmen, and to a host of Tasmanians who sensed that here was a man who could tell them more about their unknown wilderness than almost anyone before him. People were not slow to see that he differed from the remembered images of our sturdy pioneers whose feats as axemen, roadbuilders, explorers or mining prospectors were formidable, but whose love for the land was often little or none. He was certainly as tough as they had been. This was implicit in the pictures he had taken of places rugged beyond doubt. But he did not dwell upon this: he spoke of the great beauty of the wilderness, and of its primal splendour. He spoke modestly, simply. The magic of the South-West was his theme. Those who heard him came under his spell. Here, then, was the man who was to become a prime force in people's minds to resist the alienation of it. He had, mentally and physically, everything required for the arduous and compelling role he finally chose.

Seen in retrospect, his life was in every sense a preparation for it. Born in Siauliai, Lithuania in 1923, he had seen his small country overrun by the Russians in 1940, the Nazis in 1941, and by the Russians again in 1945 as they drove out the Germans. He fought the invaders as a member of the Lithuanian Resistance Movement; lived to see nearly a third of his countrymen killed or sent to concentration camps, then was angered and humiliated to find his country handed over to the USSR at the 1945 Yalta meeting between Stalin, Churchill and a dying Roosevelt. Lithuania became a Soviet State. Truchanas left it—never to return.

He and members of his family fled to Western Germany—then controlled by Allied occupation forces—and met there by prearrangement. After reaching Munich, Olegas gained admittance to its University to study law. However, Communist infiltration, agitation, and riots forced the Americans to close the buildings, and students were sent to camps for displaced persons. About this time he began to ski and climb in the Bavarian Alps. He also took an interest in the famous Bavarian mountain photographers, whose distinctive style was to influence him for the next twenty-five years.

Long before he left Europe he stood out from the crowd. This is recalled in a letter from a fellow student of the University days. "If you met him in the University grounds early in the morning and greeted him with the usual 'How are you?' you would get his answer, 'Well, but hungry.' We all were hungry most of that postwar time, but Olegas more than anyone else, for he was well-built, healthy and physically a very strong man. He used to swim in the . . . River Isar which flowed through the University grounds."

"In early Spring," continued his friend, "most of us Lithuanians watched the flowing Isar and enjoyed the warm sun, sitting on the western bank. The Isar . . . was turbulent; its swirling, muddy waters were full of round ice-blocks, heaps of snow, tree branches and usual matter which flowed at the thaw. Someone shouted, 'Who dares to swim across for a bet?' Olegas agreed to swim across and back for a loaf of bread. We his close friends were aghast, and asked him not to risk it, but he would not listen to us. He stripped, and in seconds was in the water strongly swimming across, smartly avoiding ice-blocks. When he reached the other bank he had a few moments rest, and swam . . . he was all blue from cold, his body was covered in bruises, but he was as happy as a lark; he showed his strength and ability and was one loaf richer."[2]

He came to Tasmania as a migrant, subject to the then conditions of the Commonwealth government: two years' work was required, either in industry or public works as directed. Fares from Europe were provided, subject to repayment. He began work with the Electrolytic Zinc Company at Risdon near Hobart. He and others were set to pushing old trucks loaded with metal along worn and rusty rails. Olegas had more than enough time to regret his unfinished law degree as he slowly became used to the heavy, dirty work. When his two-year term was near its end he wryly told his friends that he was now a "professional pusher."[3]

By now, his father, mother and sister had arrived in Hobart as migrants, sponsored by Olegas and his brother-in-law. He had much to tell them about their new country, so different from Lithuania with its ancient Indo-Germanic language and rich history. Truchanas told his family that Tasmania had been founded as a penal colony less than one hundred and fifty years before their arrival. Convicts from Britain had laid its foundations. It had been a land to be cleared for pasture—a land regarded as hostile by those who sought to subdue it. Only the Aborigines had lived in harmony with it, taking what it offered, asking nothing more. Within a few decades their numbers were at low ebb. They were hunted from their tribal lands—often into war with neighbours they had respected for centuries. White settlers had little time and less inclination to understand the problems of the black natives. Belated efforts to save them failed utterly. By 1878 they were extinct.

Meanwhile, the island prospered. Transportation of convicts ceased. More free settlers arrived, ready to work hard to establish themselves, twelve thousand miles from their homeland. They found some solace in the imitation of English architecture and gardens; it seemed an assurance of continuity of cherished things, and an insurance against the real or imagined intrusion of the bush with its unfamiliar trees and impossible animals. "A trip back home to the old country" was a phrase that lingered until just a few decades ago, and repeated even by those Tasmanian-born who had never left their island. Small wonder, then, that love of this island came late—to some not at all, even to this day.

Olegas Truchanas discovered that Tasmania (with its hawthorn hedges, stone bridges and Georgian houses) was advertised as "This Other England," that the convict ruins at Port Arthur drew thousands; that people went to the highland lakes for trout fishing, but, incredibly, the largest unspoiled part of the island, the South-West, lay neglected. It was still only roughly mapped, crammed with mountains, many unclimbed, even unnamed. Lakes and tarns abounded, rivers and creeks from a thousand valleys found their way to a coast that remained as wild as it was when Tasman first sighted the twin peaks of Heemskirk and Zeehan in 1642.

He found that few Tasmanians knew much about the South-West of their State, and fewer cared about its future. If mentioned at all, it was in terms of possible mineral wealth or hydroelectric potential. The one point on which many agreed was that it was unfit for human habitation. The coast, it was said, was wild and treacherous. The rain forests of the deep ravines were so nearly impenetrable that shipwrecked seamen had almost no chance of getting through to any settled area beyond. Convict escapees from the penal settlement at Macquarie Harbour were recaptured or lost. One killed his mates for food. Besides this, they said, rain fell almost incessantly or a sudden storm could appear out of a blue sky bringing snow, hail or sleet, carried by gale-force winds. Only bushwalkers or mining prospectors knew much about the region, and most of it remained a mystery.

It was this mystery, and its wild beauty that touched Truchanas—perhaps also, its challenge. It delighted him to think of the undiscovered places he might visit. Every inch of Europe, he said, must have been trodden by some man at some time. In the South-West, he thought, he could perhaps find lakes, tarns, or a river that he would be the first to see. And so began the long treks, the lone journeys when he disappeared for weeks into this region of some five thousand square miles of practically uninhabited land, to emerge each time with more knowledge, and with what was of greater significance—more photographs.

He already had an impressive knowledge of photography—some of it gained from his association with the Bavarian alpine photographers. Their clubs and societies demanded and achieved the high standard of photographic art that made them justly famous. His time with them was short but valuable. There is no doubt that Truchanas gained fundamental knowledge in the techniques of mountain photography, on which he built his own distinctive style. It must be said however that this experience was but a catalyst to spark off the latent talent, the intuitive artist.

Olegas Truchanas had artistic insight to a marked degree, and his finest works have a power few have equalled. His earlier work was monochrome—colour came later. It won him prizes and acclaim in Australia and overseas. There is no doubt that monochrome work provided a basis for his colour photography. Monochrome depends greatly on quality of tone—a rich variety of greys from black to white. Light, shade and texture are principal considerations. Clarity of form must be realised within the limitations of monochrome without the assistance of colour. For him, colour was to merely enhance the already established tonal pattern of his pictures. His sensitivity

ILLUS. 2 *Munich 1947*

to subtle tonality infuses his work so strongly that it has, in fact, the "Truchanas look"—the style of the man.

The South-West wilderness seemed to him essentially a tonal landscape of rich, dramatic, changing effects of light on the basic landforms. Shadows, cast by processions of clouds, move across his landscapes; mountains or valleys are lit by the sun or edged in sombre shade. Long twilights and slow dawns gave scope for his art, for his poetic nature.

During his earlier years in Tasmania his patience was notable. He once built a stone cairn in a narrow gully to use as a vantage point to photograph a dead tree seen against the sky at the end of the gully. The sky was cloudless, and he needed cloud in an area to balance his composition, and to intensify the mood. He waited, seated on the rockpile, reading until conditions were exactly right for his picture. Two hours had passed. Many of his best black and white works were the result of this kind of careful planning, followed by countless hours in his darkroom. He often went there in the early evening to emerge at dawn holding one print.

Travelling alone in the South-West made it possible for him to pause for an hour or two, to allow a shadow to lengthen, mists to rise, or some eminence to emerge into light. He knew, like most artists, that silence and meditation are the true sources of revelation; his photographs confirm it.

2 *Forest Veteran*

2

ON APRIL 12, 1928, A HOBART NEWSPAPER, *The Mercury*, printed the result of an interview with members of a party just returned from a prospect of the Gordon River. The headlines were bold, the tone enthusiastic:

THE GORDON RIVER
Exploration of "The Splits"
"The Show Place of Tasmania"
Sprent Falls Alone Worth the Trip

Olegas Truchanas found this report during his early years in Tasmania. It stated that with the return of the prospectors Messrs J. H. Sticht, G. W. Harrison and C. Abel had come the first reliable information regarding that section of the Gordon River formerly known as "The Gorge" but now appropriately named "The Splits." It continued: "The portion of the waterway referred to is that which for many years was believed to flow through a huge tunnel in the mountain. The rocky slopes rise precipitously on either side for hundreds of feet, and viewed from downstream present the appearance of the river flowing through an underground passage.

"This conception was disproved some years ago, when Messrs C. Abel and C. Doherty, who were able to get within a short distance of the spot, discovered that such was not the case. Messrs Sticht and Harrison, accompanied by Mr C. Abel, owing to the exceptionally favourable conditions, succeeded in their arduous and extremely hazardous task of making a complete examination of this remarkable section of the river. They have been where no other man has been. They found the water of the river lower than it has ever been known to be, due to the abnormally long and dry summer, and this facilitated their progress.

"In order to accomplish their task they had to scale cliffs, crawl round narrow ledges, wade through swirling water, walk over rock faces of every conceivable shape, and polished as smooth as glass, and risk the possibility of the river rising and preventing their return."[4] Sticht declared The Splits to be "wonderful; marvellous; words can scarcely describe the glory of the place. I am certain there is nothing to equal them in Tasmania . . . The first split consists of two basins connected by three chambers and is most striking, being overhung by a cliff. The water is very deep. The second is covered with huge rocks and whirlpools. It is not possible to get into these basins except by means of a rope . . . in time to come they will be visited by thousands of people annually."[5]

The men who went there in 1928 could not have foreseen that almost thirty years later, a young Lithuanian, inspired by their story, would navigate this most mysterious stretch of the Gordon that they had only glimpsed, and be the first to do so; that he would confirm many of their observations, and disprove others; that he would discover major errors on official maps, and with great accuracy, rectify the errors; that he would bring back information about places long shrouded in mystery. He had all the qualities needed to undertake the first navigation of this river. He could swim like an otter, was an experienced bushman and mountaineer, and used to handling small boats. The key to a successful journey down this river would be determined by the choice of the right kind of craft.

He designed a kayak specially for the venture. The frame of the canoe was of aluminium strips, no part longer than six feet. It could be assembled or dismantled at will by using a system of bolts. Once assembled, a canvas cover was slipped over the frame like a glove. Neatly packaged, it could be easily stowed in a light aircraft, or during a difficult journey it could be dismantled and carried.

His plan for the attempt was novel. The first stage involved a flight by light aircraft to Lake Pedder, where he could be landed, complete with gear and packaged kayak on its wide beach. The second stage was to paddle across the lake to its western shore where the Serpentine River began its journey to the Gordon, firstly by a leisurely winding course across a button-grass plain, and then entering a gorge that led it to the Gordon over a series of waterfalls and rapids with a spectacular drop of six hundred feet in the last mile. The second stage was not completed. A few days after his departure from Lake Pedder in December 1954, he had almost reached the junction with the Gordon when he lost his canoe and most of his equipment. Torrential rain had fallen the night before. The rising waters made his craft difficult to manage.

At the top of a twenty foot waterfall, the canoe was drawn under a huge rock in mid-stream and wrapped around it. Truchanas, parted from his kayak, went over the fall, but was suspended by a rope, one end of it fastened to his belt, the other to the canoe. He was now in the centre of the waterfall, unable to move, even to climb back up the rope against the tremendous weight of water falling on his body. Suddenly the belt-fitting snapped, and he dropped into the seething pool below, to be swept down-stream to finally emerge and climb ashore. The canoe could not be freed, and much of his gear was in it. But a pack containing his sleeping-bag, tent, camera, and a book was saved. The book was Apsley Cherry Garrard's *The Worst Journey in the World*.

He had left an emergency food supply on a high hill nearby, but this good strategy was marred by an event quite unexpected. In his struggle with the deluge, he lost his trousers. A bare-legged retreat across the wild country was unthinkable. Holding his parka upside down he thought of a way to avoid this. "I pushed my legs through its sleeves, and tied it round the waist with a piece of string. It is very necessary to take care of one's legs in these parts. It took considerable effort to climb out of the gorge to the emergency depot."[6] During his five day return journey by way of Detached Peak he built a cairn on a summit to mark the occasion. Of this he dryly remarked "probably not many summits have been reached by men without trousers."[7] He reached Lake Pedder a day later and was delighted to find a light aircraft, piloted by Mr Lloyd Jones, on the beach. Truchanas was safely back in Hobart within an hour.

I met him that same afternon travelling on a suburban bus as its only passenger. He boarded it when it stopped near his house and came directly to me—his face creased in the unmistakable Truchanas grin. As the bus rattled towards the city, he told me the story of the "shipwreck" in the Serpentine gorge. No man delighted more in telling a story against himself. I looked at his immaculate sports suit and polished shoes, and found it hard to believe that only a few hours before he had been on the beach at Lake Pedder, facing a further three days' march to the nearest habitation.

It was three years before the next attempt was made. This time it was successful, but not without incident. After all, a river that had resisted complete exploration for more than a century and a half could be expected to present difficulties of the most formidable kind. He had improved the design of the kayak, and that of an aluminium twin-bladed paddle. He also incorporated various safety devices. Again, as in the first journey he began his journey at Lake Pedder.

Heavy rain set in, impeding his passage through the Serpentine gorge, but he reached the junction at the Gordon without mishap—this time dismantling his kayak to get around difficult waterfalls, rapids and rocks. The journey down the Gordon was interrupted by capsizes in large rapids, and more waterfalls required laborious portage over and around huge boulders. At one place he passed through a large tunnel-like hole under some rocks. He was now approaching the area partly explored by the Sticht party in 1928. He negotiated a small rocky gorge "up from the Albert River junction where the Gordon makes a prominent loop."[8] He thought it not unreasonable to judge it another "Split" quite distinct from those known: He climbed the hills on the left bank of the Gordon to photograph it and "to see if there was enough ground to use there in future airdrops, and to test my theory that Messrs Harrison, Sticht and Abel must have climbed these hills in 1928 mistaking them for the Wilmot Range. Did they mistake the Albert River for the Serpentine? Could one possibly see Lake Pedder from these summits as they claimed? The answer: they could not."[9]

He had trouble in the region of the Splits. The water was higher than normal, and "steep blade-like buttresses of polished rock forming narrow channels containing waterfalls"[10] forced him to dismantle his canoe and repack it for portage round them. Over several days, he made a careful reconnaissance of the Splits, and from the water photographed this "incredible place" for the first time. During his forays in the area, he discovered a long abandoned track "on the right bank high along the top of a ridge flanking the first Split (Upper)."[11]

Above the Sprent River junction he saw "high on the bank of the Gordon, the remnants of the stables and huts built by the piners before the end of the century."[12] "These ruins," he declared, "appear to have been wrecked by a flood of unusual magnitude. It must have been the same flood which carried away most of Pyramid Island, transforming an island carrying large trees growing in much loose rock and soil into a flat slab of bare bedrock only a few feet above water."[13] The final

ILLUS. 3 *Adjusting the load*

PETER DOMBROVSKIS

act of his journey occurred upon reaching Macquarie Harbour. He spent a night on Sarah Island, "to test the theory of the presence of ghosts at this cruel and lonely place."[14] Next morning he stepped into his kayak and began the leisurely trip across the broad expanse of water towards his destination, Strahan.

His short diary does not record the most exhausting episode—the overland climb to avoid the Splits—a passage through them was impossible. On the first day he carried his tent and camping gear up the mountainside and camped the night. Next morning he scrambled back down to the place he had left his kayak, dismantled it, packed and carried its fifty-five pound weight up to and beyond his camp, pushing on as far as time would allow, to drop the craft and return to the camp for the night. This routine was repeated for several days until everything was safely back at river level on the downstream side of the mountain ranges.

We get some idea of the difficulties in pushing through scrub in this country from the 1928 report. "A track had to be cut over the Wilmot Range with its dense forest of horizontal and bauera. The eastern side of the mountain is terraced with small cliffs from ten to twenty feet high. The horizontal was literally matted together. We had to either walk over the top, and this we did in some places for a good distance, or crawl along the ground."[15]

A further hazard is the constant threat—mentioned in the 1928 report but not by Truchanas— of sudden rain, perhaps far upstream, which can send water racing down to trap the unwary. "In the Splits the flood water mark is easily one hundred feet above Summer level of the river. How wonderful must be the sight of this river in flood! A body of water one hundred feet deep, froth and foam covered, hurtling through deep ravines, with thunder-like roar. The mighty swirl and swish of the whirlpool gouging away the bank, tearing limbs from trees and up-rooting monarchs of the forest. It is grand, but forbidding. Neither man nor beast must venture on its surface in these upper reaches. Buoyant pine logs floating down suddenly disappear sucked down by mammoth whirlpools, reappearing again some distance downstream. This is the river in its angry mood."[16]

It is hard to believe all this when one sees the tranquil surface of the Gordon estuary from the deck of a tourist launch. Spent of the fury of its confinement further upstream, it mirrors the towering rain-forest on a surface that appears nearly motionless. The voyage from Strahan across Macquarie Harbour to the estuary is famous throughout the nation, but to Sticht, it was the area beyond the navigable estuary that held the finest scenery, "the grandeur of it greatly surpassing that of the lower reaches of the river."[17]

ILLUS. 4   *First Split, Gordon River from the air*

3

BETWEEN THE TWO CANOE voyages, in 1956, he married Melva Stocks whom he met in Launceston some five years earlier when she was a member of the Launceston Walking Club. He had been invited to talk to members about his solo climb of Federation Peak. She recalls their first meeting. "As he came towards us there was no doubting who he was—the strong face, the bushwalker's stride, the beam of pleasure. But mixed with this was a great shyness and a certain formality."[18]

The house he built on a steep site at Forest Road, West Hobart, was a model of precision. The foundation was built from large sandstone blocks, convict hewn, and recovered from a demolished building. Where some stones had to be recut to fit the plan of the house, Truchanas refaced and matched them to the mason's chisel marks of a century earlier. His skill with woodwork and joinery was remarkable; the interior of the house showed craftsmanship rarely equalled by the rough and ready builders in that post-war boom. The steep-sloped land was carefully terraced, then planted with native trees and shrubs, together with some European kinds—in all, more than two hundred species. The house became a meeting place for friends who gathered around the couple; a common interest in natural things, and the sharing of this through the agency of the camera, was the core of it all.

ILLUS. 5 *"Snow-caving" Anita with Nicholas—Rima above*

These were good years. Two daughters were born, Anita and Rima. As a family they walked and camped in summer and went to the snowfields to ski in winter. The children were taught to become self-reliant. They were shown how to behave if lost. Each of them carried a small whistle fastened to a lanyard. It seemed perhaps a natural step from family to community in this kind of education. Truchanas was impressed by the work done by the National Fitness Council in the establishment of its Adventure Camps for boys, which trained youths in outdoor activities. He became an instructor in the art of canoeing, taking part in week-end and holiday periods for canoe and camping expeditions along Tasmanian rivers. The youngsters trusted this man with the soft voice and strange accent, who did not boast, nor asked of them anything he could not do himself. He explained things carefully, patiently and quietly. He made clear that physical fitness was sought not as an end in itself, but as a bonus from an active life in natural surroundings enjoyed for its own sake. His influence was immeasurable.

His body was powerful with a line and form, not of the gymnasium, but of the land with its constant invitation to move over it without fuss, and with respect. In his maxims for bushcraft he said, "Bushwhacking is not thrashing about in thick scrub hoping for the best; nor is it taking a blind stab at an entirely unknown stretch of wilderness, and expecting somehow to get out before dark . . . it is to go places with as little interference as possible, without becoming tangled up in impossible 'going' . . . The idea is to ease one's way through, over, under, and around obstacles. Let those who get satisfaction out of fighting everything in their way do it. Keep well behind though, for when they push through, something is going to swing back and get you somewhere— usually across the face."[19]

"For us as for animals," he claimed, "an ability to find our way in the wilderness is not so much a development of the intellect as it is the sharpening of the senses . . . the awakening of reactions to the terrain, together with the capacity to catalogue these mental compounds of sights, sounds, smells and feeling, so as to be able to identify them later in relation to the surroundings that gave rise to them. Bushcraft," he added, "calls for a continuous observation and consideration of the drainage slope upon which you are walking. The faint suggestion of a little swale as you descend calls for a prompt decision as to your course, for it will shortly widen into a gully, then into a ravine, and finally becomes a valley; in another mile or so hours may be required to cross it in rectifying an error that could originally have been prevented by a few steps."[20]

When it came to camp-sites he was scrupulous. He insisted that so far as possible, no sign of habitation should remain when his party left. After burial of all waste, sites were swept clean with improvised brooms. He resented some people's thoughtless and destructive attitudes to bush and countryside—"They are savages; they plant zinnias in their gardens, mow and trim their lawns, then go out and throw beer-cans and rubbish all over the place; they do not love their country."[21]

Early experiences in Tasmanian bush taught him much. In 1948 he had still to learn of the notorious horizontal scrub and bauera. Nothing of his experience in Lithuania or Germany could have helped him with these. Horizontal scrub derives its name from its habit of first growing upright on long thin stems to a height of forty or forty-five feet, and then, being unable to support itself, literally lies down horizontally. At once, a change occurs. The stems, once bare of foliage except for a crown of leaves at the top, now send up fresh vertical shoots. The whole process is repeated interminably until a mat of utmost confusion results. This often impenetrable forest can reach a height of more than one hundred feet in a deep gully. Even with a machete, a strong man is fortunate if he progresses more than a few hundred yards in a day. Rain, mosquitoes and leeches often add finishing touches to a dismal canvas.

It was this kind of forest, among other things, that delayed the successful ascent of Federation Peak for nearly half a century after its discovery in 1901. Tough and experienced Tasmanians had made determined attempts to reach it, and in 1947 a party came within six hundred feet of the summit; they returned with information which they freely passed on to others. In 1949, a party from Geelong College (Victoria) led by John Bechervaise succeeded in climbing it for the first time. Three hundred feet of rope was carried and used by the final party of four to assist in the climbing of the last difficult stage. From the summit Lake Geeves could be seen below their feet, at the end of a two thousand foot vertical drop. It became clear to all involved, that personal determination and luck with the weather were the two most important factors of the exercise.

Characteristically, Truchanas decided to make the attempt alone. In 1952, he set off with a seventy pound pack and succeeded in reaching the summit. The time taken for the ascent and return was twenty-eight days. It was, as expected, a slow and tedious process, but to him infinitely worthwhile. Afterwards he made his first public screening of the exciting photographs he brought back.

He determined to try to find an easier route. This time he flew with a friend, John De Bavay, to the south coast of Tasmania. De Bavay said, "Lloyd Jones flew us into Cox's Bight, but *en route* Olegas made two food drops, one at Goon Moor for the home journey, and one at Hanging Lake for our activities around Federation Peak. Lloyd set us down on the beach at Cox's Bight."[22] The two men climbed nearby mountains to look around and plan their route, and discovered a promising lead along a ridge which struck northward. It was then they came close to disaster. They met violent weather—a westerly gale drove in the rain horizontally forcing them to seek cover in the lee of a rock. "Our fingers," said De Bavay, "were too cold to open our packs of food. The weather abating a little we pushed along the ridge, which consisted of a series of elevations, on which we caught the full force of the storm, and a series of saddles with some of the highest, densest, toughest scoparia that either of us had ever met. It was on an exposed ridge and we couldn't get off it. There was no place to camp, and we had not eaten for hours. Olegas with his superior stamina, was out in front but he, like me, was feeling the strain of this ordeal."[23]

That afternoon De Bavay, an experienced bushwalker, collapsed from exhaustion. But he observed that though Truchanas was suffering badly, "somehow he found the reserves to pitch the tent on a slanting ledge of a small cliff just ahead of us. Somehow he got me to it and into my sleeping bag, and himself into his, and then collapsed too. The tent kept the worst of the rain off us, but the water ran down the cliff and through the tent under our ground sheets. Yet uncomfortable as it was, it provided the protection without which I would not have survived. There is no doubt that Olegas saved my life."[24]

They were forced to return to the coast and were taken in by the King family at Port Davey where they rested for several days, and repaired their gear. After this, provided with food by Denis King, the intrepid pair set off to challenge Federation Peak by a slightly different route. The breakthrough came on the day they saw a high ridge that appeared to lead in the right direction. It did. De Bavay wrote, "Another day and a half we stood at the pass overlooking Hanging Lake, a beautiful sight. We had pioneered a new easy route to Federation Peak and we felt exultant."[25]

Easier? *The Mercury*, reporting the journey stated, "The climb from Port Davey was made in an effort to find an easier route to the peak, but it is now believed that there is no easy route."

4

TIME PASSED. HIS REPUTATION as a bushman, explorer, canoeist, photographer and lecturer was growing. Truchanas visited schools, societies, private homes—anywhere he could share the joy of discovery he felt about the South-West wilderness. Slide evenings, in his hands, became memorable events, a sharing of his finest works carefully prepared for the enjoyment of others. To those who saw such convincing evidence of its unspoiled grandeur, the South-West seemed to hold promise of a permanent and inexhaustible source of scenic and ecological wonder. The country slumbered on, primeval, timeless.

In 1963 there was a dramatic announcement that was to change all this. On October 24 of that year, an editorial in *The Mercury* (Hobart) was headed,

OPENING UP SOUTH-WEST

"The imagination of thinking Tasmanians," it said, "will be excited by the announcement by the Prime Minister that the Commonwealth Government will bear the cost of constructing an access road from Southern Tasmania towards the remote and hitherto almost inaccessible South-West. The primary purpose of the grant is to assist in the development of the vast hydro-electric resources known to exist in the Gordon River area." Most Tasmanians were indeed excited by the prospect of motoring into this country, so rugged that its access road was to cost five million dollars, or one hundred thousand dollars per mile to build.

There was one nagging thought in the minds of many. Would the proposed Gordon River power development include the destruction of the South-West's most priceless asset, Lake Pedder? The lake had been incorporated in a National Park gazetted nearly a decade earlier.

Surely this could not be violated? Nervous inquiries met with non-committal official replies, and as the new road wound its way into the wilderness, an equally substantial path was being built towards what would become a controversy of national magnitude.

Olegas Truchanas was dismayed. He, along with hundreds of fellow Tasmanians, was employed at the head office of the Hydro-Electric Commission, whose task it was to investigate the power potential of the area and to make recommendations to the Tasmanian Government. He was more dismayed when, in 1965, the Premier announced that "there would be some modification of Lake Pedder National Park."[26] By 1967 the "modification" included legislation to provide for the total obliteration of the lake, with its two-mile beach, under fifty feet of water.

For Truchanas, 1967 was a fateful year. Added to the sense of loss he felt at the violation of a National Park, was the shock of another event. On February 7, a great fire swept through south-eastern Tasmania. In a few short hours sixty-two people died, and over one thousand five hundred houses were destroyed, his own among them. Next day, I stood with him in the ashes. Only the chimney stood against the sky. Twisted steel girders and window frames were the only reminders of a structure. Plate glass lay in deep folds, like heavy cloth. He poked at the remains of his slide projector and said, "I can build another house—that is nothing. But I can never replace my fifteen years of photographs and my books—they are the real loss."

The good years had gone. Lake Pedder seemed doomed, and as a result, all other national parks appeared endangered. He again realised that still so few knew the value and potential of this wilderness, and fewer still had access to it except through the medium of photography—which he was fully aware, was the way to public enlightenment. But his pictures lay in ashes. Within the month he had found another house for his family and settled them in. Soon after, a son, Nicholas was born. Then began the long uphill slog to replace his work. He had just a little less than five years to live. He could not have worked harder had he known, for he left more than three thousand photographs as witness.

Landscape photography had already played an important part in making people aware of the rugged country beyond the settled valleys. Perhaps the most famous of the early professional photographers was J. W. Beattie (1859-1930). Between 1880 and 1925 he covered most of the island's coastal scenery, the central highland lake country, and the lower reaches of the west coast rivers. Others followed; many have a permanent niche in the history of Australian photography. In all this time the South-West had yielded little to the camera. Of the wilderness areas it remained the least known. The excellent works produced by the more skilled photographers among bush-walkers were not widely seen.

After World War II there was a breakthrough. Light aircraft and the 35mm. still-camera provided a combination of speed and versatility. Lloyd Jones, Tasmanian-born flying instructor, was quick to introduce aerial photography to the South-West, and by 1953 had published the first of a series of three booklets, each with colour plates of Tasmanian scenes. He championed the South-West as a potential tourist and scenic reserve. His enthusiasm fell mostly on deaf ears, and his pictures hardly raised an eyebrow among the vote-conscious government members of the day. He was too early.

However, Jones had already played an even more important role—one that was to have consequences of a spectacular kind. He discovered that it was possible to land an aircraft on the beach at Lake Pedder. He was the first pilot to do so. The gateway to the South-West was open. In December 1947, a party of walkers was put down with their gear. They were Harry Buckie, Peter Canning, Dennis Wilson and Ralph Hope-Johnstone, who took what were possibly the first colour pictures at the lake. Harry Buckie painted, Dennis Wilson made black-and-white photographs. They were the first—thousands were to follow before the rising waters closed over the whole splendid scene twenty-five years later.

ILLUS. 6 *At the Coronets, overlooking Lake Pedder 1971*   ELSPETH VAUGHAN

A new era had begun. Not only were the beach and lake beautiful beyond belief but people could now directly enter some of the finest walking country in the whole of the South-West from this place which lay at its very centre. There were easy day-walks close at hand, easy climbing country nearby, even for children, and farther south, the mighty Western Arthurs for the more experienced. Pedder seemed set for ever; its vast, solid quartz beach, large enough in summer to present an area equal to that of the city of Sydney—two miles long and six hundred to eight hundred yards wide—a natural aerodrome capable of almost unlimited light plane traffic, free of upkeep, self-renewing, in itself indestructible. It was a gift.

Twenty years later, the means for its destruction was at hand, now supported by the legislation necessary to bring it about. There were six more years of bitter controversy ahead. The issues raised were to deeply divide the people of Tasmania, draw the strongest condemnation from United Nations, and ultimately to bring about a Federal Government inquiry. The political, economic and legal uncertainty surrounding the Lake Pedder dispute is a matter that will be debated indefinitely.

One aspect of the dispute, for historians, will surely remain among the most inexplicable of all. During the years of arguments, politicians listened to evidence and made judgments on this place that in most cases they had neither seen, nor had any intention of visiting. Yet by the time the controversy had reached its height, thousands of people of all ages had flown to the lake in shuttle-service flights. Incredibly, at Parliament House, in Hobart, decisions of the gravest consequence were reached by references to maps and documents alone while the reality lay less than sixty air miles from the seat of government. Only one thing emerged with any clarity— something supremely beautiful was about to be destroyed—that issue, at least, remained simple.

Olegas Truchanas had visited Lake Pedder more than thirty times. He knew it intimately in all its moods and seasons. He knew also that no map, no description, however detailed could remotely convey the sense of awe and wonder felt by those who saw this place. Communication between those who have seen Lake Pedder and those who have not, has always been difficult and must remain so. It is like another language, beyond the reach of maps or words. As a conservationist, Truchanas believed that the Gordon scheme could, and should have proceeded without the destruction of Lake Pedder, through Government recognition of its future value. As a public servant he was expected to remain uncritical of the Government's decision to destroy the lake.

There remained one course open to him. He could show the people of Tasmania, through his photographs, what they were about to lose. They should at least know what this place was like before it vanished for ever. It was an act of moral courage at a time when the battle had been long, and tempers had grown short. The public response to his audio-visual presentations at the Hobart

Town Hall was dramatic. On eight consecutive occasions there was standing room only. So compelling were these shows, the doors of the hall had to be closed half an hour before each presentation began. Hundreds were turned away on each occasion. People came not only to see the superb quality of his pictures, but also to hear the explorer. His rich voice, his warmth, dry humour and lucid speeches will be long remembered.

The key to the successful techniques employed in the audio-visuals was provided by his long-time friend, Ralph Hope-Johnstone, an engineer with a wide knowledge of optics, electronics and music, who was deeply interested in the visual appeal of images from slides dissolving and fading to the demands of music. He set about solving the problem of recording a programme of image and sound, perfecting it in his studio, and later presenting it fully automated to a large audience. He solved the problem, built the equipment, and demonstrated its operation to a delighted Truchanas.

The subtle and mysterious beauty of Lake Pedder was viewed on a large screen by people who listened to the music of Sibelius and Delius. They watched scene after scene appear, fade and dissolve to the haunting music of the two composers. The vision of Pedder was so powerful that people who had not seen the lake were astounded that its destruction could ever have been contemplated. Some were angry or outraged; others subsided to despair. Those unwilling to visualise the destruction of the lake sometimes indulged themselves in the belief that this place was so huge, so magnificent that it would never be destroyed by human agency. Surely it could not happen?

The engineers, the dam builders, knew better—the waters would rise. They worked on. Most workers would never see Lake Pedder. The dams that were to raise the waters to create the ninety-three square mile impoundment were far from Pedder, out of sight. So, with few exceptions, neither the members of government who legislated, nor the men who built the dams were ever to see the true centre of the controversy. For those who sensed that some monumental blunder might have been made, it would be better perhaps not to see the lake at all. For those who were confused, there was always the official assurance that the new "lake" would be of far greater importance than the original. This, apart from aesthetic considerations, entirely ignored the claims of scientists throughout the world that the lake's unique ecology, still imperfectly known, was of immense value to mankind and science.

Certainly the new lake would not lack grandeur; the mountain ranges alone would provide that, but everywhere else around its shores, it would bear the mark of man's intrusion into the natural order, no matter how considerate the disguise. After the flooding, the only evidence of the beauty of this once incomparable place would reside in the photographs.

4 *Untitled*

5

THE TRAGIC LOSS OF Lake Pedder became known throughout the world. In Tasmania the concern was such that all other conservation issues were in danger of being shelved or forgotten. At this time Truchanas was engaged in another battle—unknown to the public until it was almost over, nearly two years after it began. It was the struggle to save a Huon pine forest on the Denison River, discovered by the Sticht party in 1928. His successful fight ranks among the foremost events in the history of conservation. It stands as a model for others.

Huon pine has exceptional qualities, and is eagerly sought. It grows in dense rain forest, and only in areas of the west and south-west of Tasmania. It does not grow anywhere else in the world. It requires anything from five hundred to one thousand years for a tree to reach maturity. It is ideal for shipbuilding, being easy to work, and is virtually rot-proof. During the early part of the last century, convict labour was used to fell trees to provide timber for the building of sailing-ships vital to the island's economy. They were cut down along the banks of the Gordon and its tributaries, dragged to the river, ready to be carried down by the next flood. Most of the workable stands were cut down before the middle of the last century, and the convict settlement abandoned. The dwindling trade has since been carried on by a diminishing number of men. Only isolated trees and small stands survive in the few accessible areas that still remain. The industry seemed doomed, the pine irreplaceable.

Then dramatically, helicopters and chain-saws appeared. The final assault on the last trees of this kind in the world was to begin. Only their impenetrable seclusion had saved them before. Those days were over.

Truchanas was determined that by the time the industry had collapsed there should remain a small area of Huon pine for the future. He knew which area was most desirable and why; the Gordon power scheme, when completed to Stage 2, would create a huge lake, filling the valleys and gorges with its rising waters. The lake would bring its shoreline within easy walking distance of the forest on the Denison River flat, described by Sticht. Already the howl of the chain-saw echoed along the Denison River valley as the piners worked their way towards this prime stand. There was no time to lose.

On November 11, 1968, Truchanas sent a letter to the Director of the Australian Conservation Foundation to outline the case for a reserve, and to point out the threat to it. In part, it read: "Having obtained a lease of the area they moved very quickly, with a number of men brought into the valley by helicopter, with power saws, etc. and thousands of trees were cut. I visited the Denison River Gorge just downstream from where they worked, on my way to some mountains beyond, at Christmas 1966, to find some river rapids choked with pine logs. These were caught by the rocky rapids and would be flushed down in the next downpour. The work went on steadily for two years. Whether they are still cutting them or whether they have cut them all I do not know. It is impossible to obtain any information from the Forestry Department—they simply don't seem to know.

"The pine stand on the Denison River has been the only such Huon pine forest in existence. I doubt, that even before the pining began, around 1830, has there been a forest of almost exclusively Huon pines growing in a forest of their own, like they did on the Denison.

"Some day, when the Hydro-electric project on the Gordon River Stage 2 (second to Stage 1 now under construction) is completed, the great gorge of the Denison River will be flooded, making the passage through it possible by a fairly large boat. The new lake will reach just the upper end of the gorge, where the Denison River—a magnificent stream, will enter the lake. It is just there, that the tourists will be able to see the stumps of what has been the world's last stand of Huon pines, cut in 1966-68 'to bolster Strahan's flagging economy.' "[27]

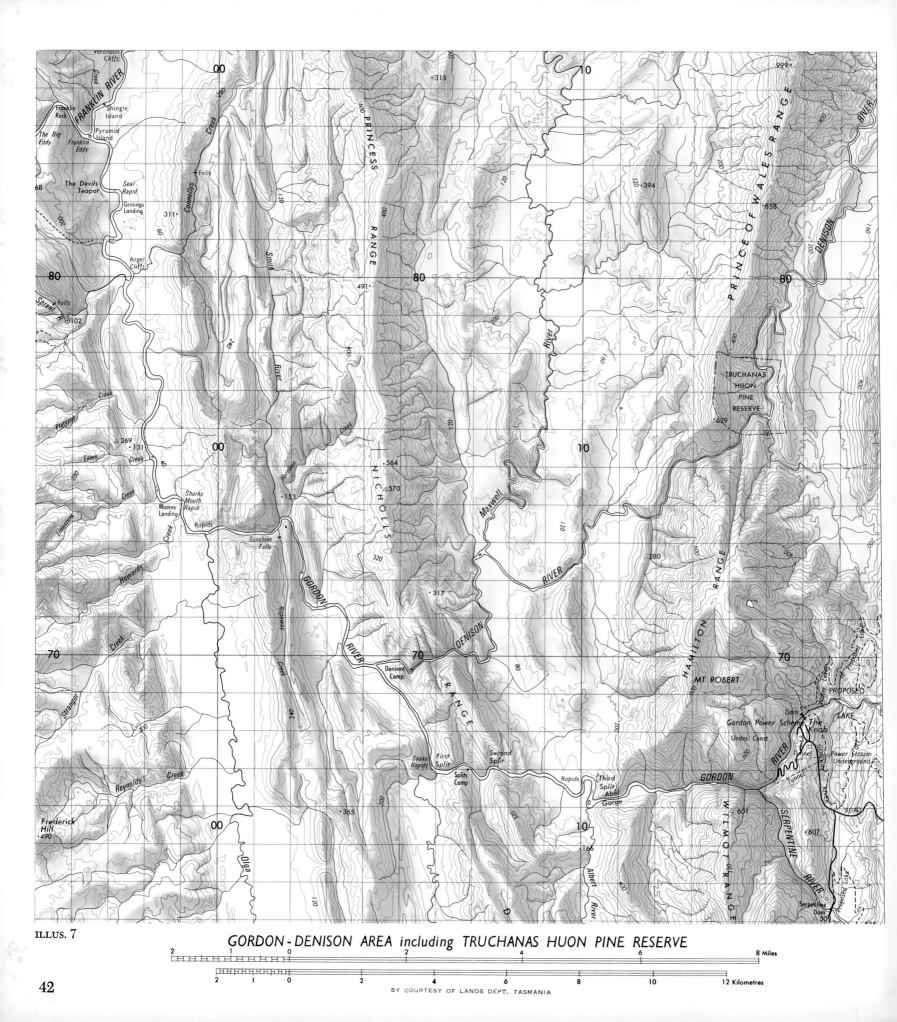

ILLUS. 7

GORDON-DENISON AREA including TRUCHANAS HUON PINE RESERVE

BY COURTESY OF LANDS DEPT. TASMANIA

At a meeting of the Tasmanian Conservation Trust in September 1969, Truchanas addressed members, with a strong plea for assistance to save the forest. Mr Louis Shoobridge, Member of the Legislative Council (and of the Trust), was sufficiently impressed to arrange a meeting with the Minister for Forests. The Minister was sympathetic to the idea that if an inspection of the proposed area revealed enough trees to warrant preservation, everything would be done to achieve this. He agreed to a request that Truchanas should be included in the party to make the survey, preferably by helicopter. Maps and documents were left with the Minister, and the Australian Conservation Foundation added its weight by writing to him, requesting that action be taken to secure this reserve without delay. Everything pointed to plain sailing. Any hope of this was short-lived, for the Forestry Commission itself was to provide the strongest resistance to what seemed to be a classic case for conservation.

On September 24, 1969, the Chief Commissioner for Forests advised his Minister that the Commission was of the opinion that the activities of the piners along the Denison River should not be terminated; any reserves of Huon pine should be sought elsewhere—it was abundant. He indicated that there was an alternative to the proposed reserve, which would in time be accessible from Lake Gordon. He provided a map showing the area suggested for the alternative reserve, and added that the Commission had accepted the advice of the piners themselves in deciding the area to be set aside; they knew the country best. He pointed out that air-photos revealed the presence of feathery-topped trees, taken to be Huon pines. He advised against air or ground inspection.

The case to save the magnificent stand of pines discovered by Sticht in 1928 seemed hopeless. Instead, the Chief Commissioner for Forests had recommended an area unknown to any but the piners, upon whose information the Commission had seemed to rely. The flimsy evidence offered by the interpretation of air-photos was inconclusive since Truchanas knew that Huon pines mostly grew under the canopy of other trees. Only close inspection by helicopter or ground search would establish proof of existence of the pines in this area. In view of the stand taken by the Chief Commissioner, the Minister for Forests, Mr E. W. Beattie, wrote to Mr Shoobridge to advise him that any further negotiations would have to be conducted with the Commission, and added that he hoped the area now proposed would be considered suitable for a reserve.

Acting upon this advice, a meeting was arranged with the Chief Commissioner. The results of this meeting are perhaps best conveyed in a report which Truchanas later sent to the Australian Conservation Foundation: "Accordingly on Wednesday the 15th (October) Dr Lake, Mr Shoobridge and myself spent an exhausting two hours with Commissioner Crane. No useful results, but at least the attitude defined. To Dr Lake, a newcomer, it must have been an experience.

We insisted on a survey without delay. He (the Chief Commissioner) refused on the grounds that there are plenty of pines anyway, as his photo-interpreter can see 'feathery tops of pines everywhere.' That it would be very costly, and serve no useful purpose as far as Forestry is concerned. etc., etc.

"We argued that we interpret from the photos that there are no pines in the proposed reserve. Dr W. Jackson, Head of the Botany Department (University of Tasmania) and by far the best informed person on this subject said there wouldn't be any. There is one corner in this reserve where pines could be found, in my opinion, but not as mature forest. Commissioner Crane agreed to lend us one of his men if we arranged the flight ourselves, but would not contribute one dollar towards helicopter costs."[28]

When the Chief Commissioner's door closed behind them, the small deputation left in anything but an optimistic mood. They conferred for a short time; some way must be found to visit the area proposed by the Chief Commissioner to establish once and for all whether there were pines in that forest. If the trees were there, even a small stand, they would probably have to accept the offer of a reserve in the area. If they were not there, in the shadows of the rain forest, Truchanas could then return to the question of saving the forest on the Denison River flat, described by Sticht.

A bold plan was decided. Truchanas knew that the Hydro-Electric Commission operated helicopters for its investigations in the Gordon River area. Perhaps the H.E.C. Commissioner could be persuaded to assist in this matter; after all, the reserve would become a part of the environment surrounding the new lake, and of decided interest to visitors to the power scheme. Next morning, Mr Shoobridge called on the Commissioner Mr (later Sir) Allan Knight to outline the case, and to ask if the H.E.C. would be prepared to assist in an air survey of the proposed area. The Commissioner agreed to look into the matter and sent for Truchanas, who supplied further details and maps. Ultimately, arrangements were completed for a flight survey, costs being shared by the Scenery Preservation Board, the Australian Conservation Foundation and the Hydro-Electric Commission. On Thursday 27th of November 1969, the helicopter took off in ideal weather conditions. The party consisted of N. Brouder, Chief Photo-Interpreter, Forestry Commission, M. G. Duncombe, Acting Secretary of the Scenery Preservation Board, and Olegas Truchanas representing the Tasmanian Conservation Trust and the Hydro-Electric Commission.

The reconnaissance was thorough, the report which followed equally so. The findings were conclusive—virtually no Huon pines in the area proposed by the Forestry Commission and only isolated trees in nearby areas. The report, in part, reads: "It appears that (in the area) groves consisting almost exclusively of Huon pines do not exist . . . Steep, densely wooded ridges surround the area separated by deep ravines through which small tributaries flow. Two major creeks, one on the western side of the Denison and one on its eastern side were flown over. The eastern creek has its upper reaches in the proposed reserve and was considered to be the most likely place where Huon pines could be found within this reserve. However, with the exception of its banks immediately above its junction with the Denison, it appeared to contain no pines at all."[29]

So, after all this, no groves, no forests of Huon pines in the proposed area and the piners still in a position to cut their way through to the Denison River flat where, according to Sticht, the real forest lay. Truchanas outlined a scheme to continue the survey without delay: "To locate and define for recommending as a suitable area for preservation it would in my opinion appear advisable to send in a small, self-contained ground party capable of travelling over very rough country. They should be landed by helicopter at the piners' camp, or alternatively, further upstream on one of the many gravelly islands, suitable for landing. The party should examine both banks and the lower reaches of all tributaries all the way down to the entrance of the Denison Gorge . . . The party would require several days to carry out this assignment. The valley is well sheltered by the mountains and the party, provided its members have genuine interest, should not be deterred by bad weather. It would not be necessary nor practicable to lift the party out by helicopter, there being no suitable landing place in the proximity of the gorge. The return to the Gordon Dam site would take about one and a half days scramble, perhaps two days in bad weather."[30]

Upon receipt of this report, flight arrangements were re-made. This time it would be no picnic. The party was to be left there to explore the area and then find its way back to the Gordon River the hard way. Two men were selected –Truchanas and Brian Collin of the Hydro-Electric Commission—both experienced bush-walkers. Tough the trip would be, yet it differed in one major respect from the previous one. This time the search would almost certainly lead them to the forest that Sticht had described in such glowing terms.

The two men were landed on an island on the Denison River and left there to explore the area. They were delighted with what they saw. Sticht had been right; magnificent specimens rose one hundred and forty feet or more from the moss-covered soil, in a forest nearly all of Huon pine, measuring over half a mile in length along the western bank of the Denison River and three hundred to four hundred yards in depth, extending back from the river. The search was over. Only a few trees had been cut, and those had grown near the river; otherwise this beautiful forest was intact. A count of annual growth-rings on one stump established an age of one thousand years.

The report was now made. It was to the point: "We unhesitatingly recommend that this grove of pines, protected by the adjoining area as delineated in the accompanying map be set aside as a scenic reserve. We make this recommendation on the following premises:

1. Without reasonable doubt the stand recommended is the only remaining stand of large mature Huon pines in Tasmania and therefore in the world.
2. The value of the recommended stand as a living asset far outweighs any commercial value as timber. Its potential scientific value to posterity and its value as a tourist asset should justify its preservation.
3. The boat-building industry would not be significantly assisted by the exploitation of this particular area of pines, nor would the livelihood of piners be in any significant measure adversely affected.
4. In all Tasmania's National Parks and Reserves there is no area exemplifying the unique characteristics of a true Huon pine forest."[31]

A copy of the report was sent to the Director of the Australian Conservation Foundation in which Truchanas wrote that the matter would be brought before the Scenery Preservation Board on the 27th of February. He pointed out this would be by far the quickest method of saving the trees and that "Trevor Brewer, the top man of the Morrison Bros. logging crew flew by helicopter into the Denison valley only four days ago. If we argue for a National Park it could take a long time and chain saws just could settle the issue quicker. At the moment we have made certain that more men and necessary drums of fuel don't fly in until the present issue is settled."[32]

The stage was now set. After the recommendation for preservation of the forest was made by the Scenery Preservation Board the slow interdepartmental work began. Truchanas could now relax a little. There remained two tasks; one was to set up boundary markers, and the other was to find a suitable place for the helicopter near the new proposed reserve so that any official party could be landed there when the need arose. The island previously used was a considerable distance from this place. A flight was arranged and Truchanas was once again flown to the Denison River. His annual leave was due and he intended to use it in the area. He had left his kayak at the place where the helicopter had landed before, and he planned after fixing the boundary markers, to paddle down the Denison and Gordon rivers to Strahan.

Once again it was not to be easy. This time the difficulties were created not by human agency, but ironically by the trees themselves. As the helicopter approached a small island near the forest, the pilot saw that several large pines were leaning out over the river, making any landing unsafe. He condemned the landing place and flew back up the river gorge to land Truchanas on the island first used, and left him alone with his canoe.

Next day Truchanas set off down the river wondering what he could do without tools to remove the tops from the overhanging trees. Then, on the river bank he saw a long abandoned piners' camp. There he found an axe worn and rusty; it would do the job. When he reached the place where the trees overhung the river he went ashore and set up camp. He climbed the trees one by one and "hacked off their offending tops." The job took two exhausting half-days. He then erected steel wires across the river at about twenty-five feet above the surface; the wires were decorated with sail-makers' offcuts of brightly coloured nylon, hanging every three feet. The piners were instructed by the Forestry Commission not to cut the trees inside this line, now so clearly marked. There could be no mistake.

A week later, from an H.E.C. camp on the lower Gordon River he sent a radio message to the H.E.C. Commissioner informing him that the island next to the pine forest was now suitable for landing. His task was now complete. He paddled once again on the lonely surface of Macquarie Harbour towards the little port of Strahan.

On July 28 of that year (1970) under the hand of His Excellency the Governor of Tasmania, Sir Edric Bastyan, a proclamation was issued to establish the reserve under the Scenery Preservation Act. It was gazetted on August 5, and declared "1,000 acres or thereabouts of Crown land, in the district of Franklin, vicinity of the Hamilton range, to be a scenic reserve to be known as the Denison River Huon Pine Scenic Reserve."[33]

Olegas Truchanas could not foresee that one day this reserve would carry his own name.

5 *Untitled*

6

TRUCHANAS WAS NOW RECOGNISED as an outstanding conservationist. He was accorded grudging respect by those who had reason to regard him as an embarrassment to their established procedures in maintaining material progress. Deep down, these people knew that his plea for a proper assessment of the value of the natural world had, somehow, to do with man's survival in it. Most disconcerting too was his constant reference to the needs of those to come, generations of people who would live in the twenty-first century. It was difficult to justify any attack on a man whose main concern was for others, and whose only defection from authority was his love for the wilderness of his adopted country.

By 1970 the audio visuals of Lake Pedder had become the chief source of enlightenment to people unable to visit the lake, and a sore trial to members of government. Truchanas always spoke calmly at these presentations, and his words were impressive. The recurring theme of his talks was that of his disappointment at the lack of vision in most political leadership. Most of all he was appalled at the apathetic and cursory consideration of matters affecting the South-West —"what they call the empty quarter, and I know to be filled with some of the world's most spectacular scenery."[34] He felt that these men, in the main, were only mildly concerned with the long term effects of their often hasty decisions. While he spoke of the future, they spoke almost always of the present, and even then, nearly always in terms of material resources, or the generating of power. The twenty-first century could look after itself.

In 1971 two distinct aspects of the concern for Lake Pedder were manifested. One was the unabated fight to try to persuade the Tasmanian Government to review its decision to flood the lake, and the other was a growing feeling that the summer of that year could well be the last for the lake. There was a sharpened awareness of the place itself, as there will be in the presence of any imminent death.

People flew in, walked in, to arrive at the beach just to enjoy it; to take photographs, to paint, to stroll on the beach for the last time, or just lie on the hot sand of the dunes, gazing up to the blue sky through an interlace of leaves; tea-tree, banksia, melaleuca, eucalypt. On an evening when there was a moon, parties linked arms to walk in silhouette against its light, to cross the immense level surface of the beach, singing, talking, and with closed eyes, try to guess how many minutes it would take to reach the water's edge; the edge that was hardly there at all, blending softly with the level sand.

Next morning would bring more people from Hobart. The first planes left at daybreak and campers at breakfast watched them land on the beach, one after another. Groups of walkers set off for the day, to climb nearby mountains. A documentary film was made. Clap-boards echoed, microphones were tested, and sound-technicians cursed the noise of revving planes. In the afternoon people bathed in Maria creek or the sun-warmed shallow lake, careful of sunburn at this nine hundred and sixty foot altitude. The whole spectacle was magnificent, its destruction unimaginable.

ILLUS. 8   *Final Summer*

Truchanas felt the impending loss of Pedder more than most; he knew the place better than most. He became inextricably identified with its spirit, its fate. His audio-visuals, his lectures, were the last passionate pleas of the man. On November 19, 1971 he was asked to open an exhibition of paintings, with Lake Pedder as its theme. It was during this address that he made his now celebrated speech in support of conservation: "Tasmania is not the only place in the world where long-term, careful argument has been defeated by short-term economic advantage. When we look round, the time is rapidly approaching when natural environment, natural unspoiled vistas are sadly beginning to look like left-overs from a vanishing world. This vanishing world is beautiful beyond our dreams and contains in itself rewards and gratifications never found in artificial landscape, or man-made objects, so often regarded as exciting evidence of a new world in the making."

"The natural world," he said, "contains an unbelievable diversity, and offers a variety of choices, provided of course that we retain some of this world and that we live in the manner that permits us to go out, seek it, find it, and make these choices. We must try to retain as much as possible of what still remains of the unique, rare and beautiful. It is terribly important that we take interest in the future of our remaining wilderness, and in the future of our National Parks. Is there any reason why, given this interest, and given enlightened leadership, the ideal of beauty could not become an accepted goal of national policy? Is there any reason why Tasmania should not be more beautiful on the day we leave it, than on the day we came? We don't know what the requirements of those who come after us will be. Tasmania is slowly evolving towards goals we cannot now see. If we can revise our attitudes towards the land under our feet; if we can accept a role of steward and depart from the role of conqueror; if we can accept the view that man and nature are inseparable parts of the unified whole—then Tasmania can be a shining beacon in a dull, uniform and largely artificial world."[35]

Unlike his other public lectures, at which he spoke without notes, this speech was written. It stands as a record of his wisdom and the depth of his understanding. In time, no doubt, environmental control will be exercised by governments using data processing by computer, and conservation will have ceased to be the concern of "irresponsible minorities." Truchanas, had he lived, would have provided much of this data. He earned the respect of even his opponents because of his clear thinking and practical sense of affairs. In argument he was found always to have done his homework. As a council member of the Australian Conservation Foundation, he provided reliable and complete evidence on the problems facing Tasmania in the proper development of its resources.

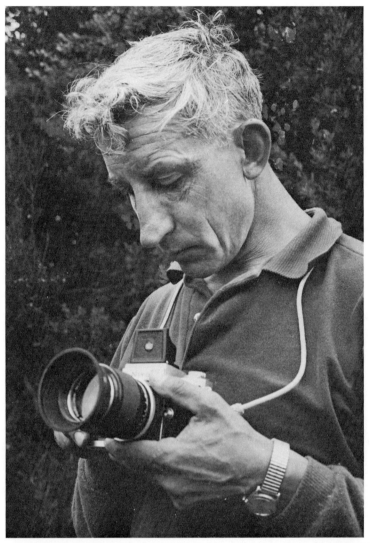

ILLUS. 9 *Portrait*

NORMAN LAIRD

He did not spare conservationists who were not willing to work hard to provide practical solutions. A note book found in his desk implies this criticism: "It is no good having idealistic solutions that just will not work. It is no use proposing to governments things that governments just cannot do. We have to think of practical things and you may take it for granted that it is very often very difficult to find and put forward that worth-while solution—a solution that is practical and one which we could work and press for. We need innovation, and innovation is seldom a strength of government."[36]

Then, miraculously, as the year was drawing to a close, Truchanas was offered an appointment of a kind he could only have dreamt of. The post was that of Senior Tutor in the School of Education and General Studies at the Tasmanian College of Advanced Education. He would instruct student teachers in a variety of subjects based on man's relation to his natural environment. The college was still in its formative stages of imaginative planning, and the concept of such a course of study was an enlightened one. A close friend of the Truchanas family, herself on the college staff, suggested that he apply for the post. After the appointment, he said, "Girl, you have saved my life." Twenty years of unremitting toil in what was essentially a "spare time" activity had now become a vocation.

But there was work to be done, and the matter was urgent. Truchanas knew that the Lower Gordon Power Development Scheme would be the next great threat to the scenic beauty of the South-West. Once again, there would be no evaluation of it in aesthetic terms; the Gordon gorge and the incomparable "Splits" would be flooded before anyone knew what had been lost. Only the photographs could show people what was there. He had no doubt of their power to convey the splendour of the place. He had seen this in 1958 when he showed his Gordon gorge pictures to Hobart audiences. Those pictures were gone—lost in the 1967 fire. He must go there again, back down the Gordon with its waterfalls and seething rapids, to the back-breaking climb over high ridges and struggles with the almost invincible bush.

He had just enough time, he thought, to do this before he commenced duties in his new appointment in February. At Christmas he would take his family to Lake Pedder as he had for the previous five years. After that—the Gordon. He spoke to a friend before leaving: "I don't want to do this trip—it is difficult and exhausting. I am tired and I am no longer young."[37] Not until much later did we all realise that the five years since the fire had exhausted him physically and spiritually. The loss of his photographs with his house in 1967, and the enormous task of trying to replace them, the loss of Lake Pedder, the long nights at his desk writing reports, mapping, studying—the audio-visuals with their lectures, his daily job, the fight for the Huon pine reserve, and the many calls innocently made on his time and energy by friends wanting advice or help, had no doubt taken their toll.

On January 6, 1972, Truchanas set off for the last time to his beloved Gordon River. This time he had no need to begin from Lake Pedder; he could now go directly to the river by the road built by the Hydro-Electric Commission as access to the power scheme. He was driven by car to the launching place by Kevin Kiernan, a young man he had met during his holiday at Lake Pedder. As a speleologist, Kiernan was interested in the limestone cliffs in the Gordon gorge, and had once tried to walk in across the Hamilton Range to the Splits, without success. Truchanas offered to show him some outstanding limestone formations not far downstream from the point of departure. After this Kiernan would walk back up the rough track made by H.E.C. hydrographers and return to Hobart that night. Truchanas would continue on alone, as before, to the Splits and on to Strahan. Tragically, this was not to be.

Truchanas had paddled across the river in his kayak to take a photograph of a native plant. The river at this point was deep and formed a large pool—a small rapid entered it from upstream and a waterfall fell away from its downstream end, between two large rocks and close to the bank. He had returned to the side of the river where all his gear had been stacked, ready for portage around a huge boulder that overhung the waterfall. He stepped ashore, and the unladen kayak overturned in a little turbulence. Standing on a rock near the waterfall, he hauled on his canoe rope to pull the craft into a quiet eddy. He slipped on the water-worn rock, smooth as glass, and wet from the previous night's rain, into the river immediately above the fall, and disappeared.

Kevin Kiernan expected to see this powerful swimmer emerge from the river within a few yards of his entry, but he watched in vain. Distraught, he ran up and down the river bank hoping to see some sign of him. None came. He raced back to his car and drove up the steep winding road back to the H.E.C. camp near the dam site, seeking help. They searched for three days; police, H.E.C. workers, skin-divers, canoeists and bushwalkers all took part. As hope faded we all had time to think about this man. When he was found, the tributes poured in; all newspapers in Tasmania honoured his work. One of the finest tributes came from the head of the Police Search and Rescue Squad (Inspector T. E. Howard) who said, "Olegas was a man who never gave up. He never spared himself. On searches he would always press on, hardly stopping to eat. He was the one man we always had to call in on important, difficult searches."[38]

Now the situation was reversed and a small army of men were doing the same for him. Among them was Peter Dombrovskis, a young man whom Olegas had taught the art of canoeing and the use of the camera. He remembers that on the third day it was decided to build a rock dam further upstream to help locate the missing man. The water would be held back temporarily, the rock and rubble pushed across the river, using bull-dozers and other earth-moving equipment. When the water level fell, on the downstream side, perhaps they would be able to see him.

The great yellow machines clanked and shuddered as they moved the rock into position. The stink of diesel fumes and clouds of rising dust filled the gorge. The day became an agony of sound. At last it was finished. Silence, almost complete; only the gurgle of the receding water marked the seconds, the minutes. They waited.

Peter Dombrovskis saw him first. Thrown against the sunken tree that lay across the river, his body had almost embraced it, his arms outstretched across its black and glistening surface.

He had been destroyed, with Biblical simplicity, by two of the elements: fire, and water. Five years had passed between their brief and terrible visits. He had perished in the river he sought to save. Classical mythology affords no stronger example of the drama of the incorruptible man who passes into legend.

PHOTO: RALPH HOPE-JOHNSTONE

ILLUS. 10

Colour plates

The mountains

George Bass (1770–1803) the explorer, wrote what is perhaps the most graphic description of Tasmania's South-West, which he and Matthew Flinders viewed from the sea. It showed, he said, "a rugged and determined front to the icy regions of the South Pole. To a very unusual elevation is added an irregularity of form that justly entitles it to rank among the foremost of the grand and wildly magnificent scenes of nature."

PLATE 1 *Western Arthur Range from near Moraine E*

58

PLATE 2 *Arthur Range skyline from the ridge between Mount Taurus and Mount Scorp*

...ith Lake Minas in middle distance

PLATE 3   *From the Frankland Range looking south toward the Arthur Range*   63

PLATE 4 *Mount Curly from Conical Mountain with Denison Range (top right) and*

Vylds Craig (top left). Lake Curly lies in the shrouded valley below

PLATE 5 *Eastern face of Mount Anne, with King William Pines (Athrotaxis selaginoides) in foreground*

PLATE 6   *Eastern Arthur Range and Federation Peak from Western Arthurs*

70

PLATE 7 *Northern face of Federation Peak from the air (4,010 feet)*

PLATE 8 *Lot's Wife from the north-east ridge of Mount Anne*

Lakes and tarns

Present day air-travellers over Tasmania's western landscape seldom remain unmoved by the sight of the breath-taking opulence of its countless lakes and tarns—many of them not yet visited by European man, so remote and inaccessible have they been, perhaps even to the bygone aborigines.

PLATE 9   *Lake Curly at the foot of Mount Curly—Denison Range in distance*

PLATE 10   *Small tarn on the saddle between Mount Orion and Mount Pegasus on the Arthur Range*

78

PLATE 11 *Mount Orion and Lake Oberon, Arthur Range*

PLATE 12   *Beach at Lake Curly*

Gordon River

"The Gordon is the King of Tasmanian rivers, because, although it is not so long as the Derwent, it rolls down more water than any other stream in the island. Rising at Lake Richmond, it flows south, parallel with the Derwent for some distance, but suddenly turns west at the Great Bend, and soon enters a deep and narrow gorge. All the western rivers cut through deep rocky gorges, but the Gordon Gorge is said to be the deepest of them all. For the last 20 miles of its course the Gordon quietens down into the splendid and majestic waterway known to so many delighted voyagers. . . . Owing to the heavy rainfall our rivers carry volumes of water out of all proportion to their length and drainage area, so that when I say that the Gordon is 120 miles long, please remember that it is larger than an Australian river that stretches out four times that distance."

Charles Whitham in
Western Tasmania

82

PLATE 13 *Temperate rainforest on the banks of the Gordon River*

PLATE 14 *Gordon River, below its junction with the Serpentine River*

PLATE 15   *The First Split, Gordon River. Olegas' canoe in the shadow of the cliff*   85

PLATE 16 *River-sculptured rocks*

Lake Pedder

The photographs in this section are of a lake which no longer exists. It lies fifty feet beneath the surface of an impoundment of water twenty-five times its size, and still bearing its name.

The flooding of the vast glacial valley in which Lake Pedder rested occurred in 1972. The water thus collected was designed to add to the main storage in the Gordon river valley as part of a hydro-electric power scheme.

One important feature of the lake was its magnificent beach, formed by countless centuries of westerly winds and wave action. The beach (in reality the floor of the lake), was covered during the wet winter months to the foot of the sand dunes which formed its eastern boundary.

Each summer, as the water level dropped, the bed of the lake was revealed as a "beach" of such magnitude that it could have comfortably supported the City of Sydney on its level surface. It was two miles in length, and reached up to eight hundred yards in width in mid-summer.

As a self-renewing natural landing ground for aircraft it was beyond price. As a work of nature its haunting beauty was beyond compare. The fourteen plates in this section recall the vanished splendour of this once unique place.

PLATE 17 *Lake Pedder from Frankland Range*

90

PLATE 18   *The beach from foothills of Frankland Range*

PLATE 19 *Early morning on the beach—Coronets in background*

PLATE 20 *Lake Pedder cloud reflections*

PLATE 21 *Maria Creek, Lake Pedder*

PLATE 22 *Pedder Sand patterns*

PLATE 23   *Dwarfed Melaleuca squamea on Pedder Beach—Franklands in background*

ᴀᴛᴇ 24 *Sunday visitors at the Lake*

102

PLATE 25 *Showers, Frankland Range*

ᴬᵀᴱ 26 *Lost playground*

PLATE 27 *Frankland Peak reflected in Lake Pedder*

PLATE 28 *Approaching westerly storm*

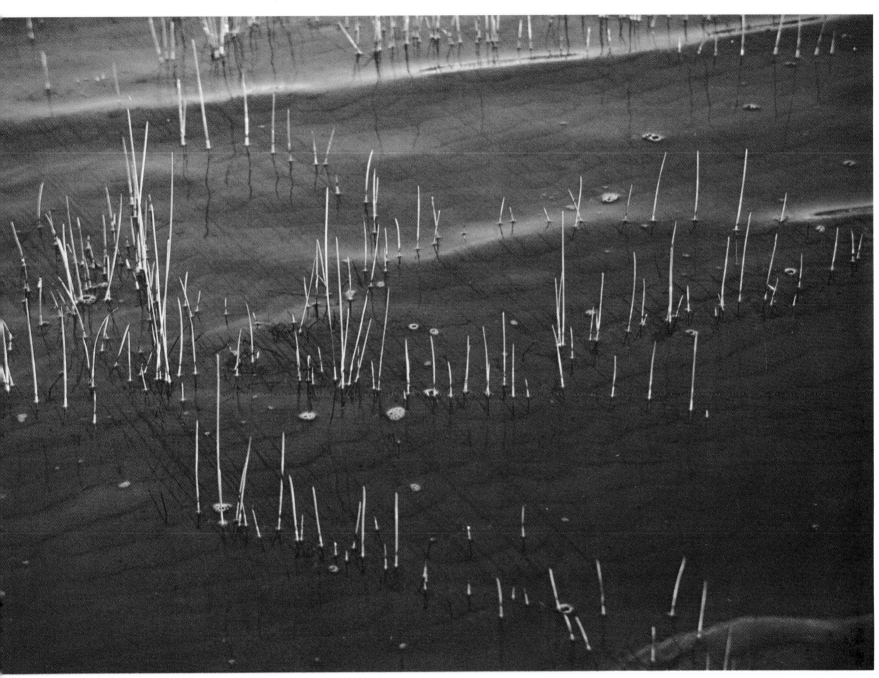

PLATE 29 *Young sedges in sandy shallows*

112

PLATE 30 *Evening—Lake Pedder*

Winter

Whilst winter is a reality in Tasmania, it is not quite the same as that experienced in northern Europe, where its onset and thaw are predictable and regular. Tasmania is an island of micro-climates. A bather standing on the warm sand at Swansea beach on the east coast may not suspect that snow may be falling at Federation Peak, a little more than a hundred miles distant, at the same moment.

"Winter" may come and go at any time. There are places, particularly above 3,000 feet, where snow patches remain well into the summer. Frost, snow and sun may combine to delight the photographer.

PLATE 31 *Snow cornice at Mount Mawson, Mount Field National Park*

PLATE 32 *Morning thaw, Tarn Shelf, Mount Field National Park*

117

118

PLATE 33 *Snow gums (Eucalyptus coccifera) and ski trails. Mount Mawson, Mount Field*

National Park

PLATE 34 *Deciduous Beech (Nothofagus gunnii) at Tarn Shelf, Mount Field National Park*

PLATE 35   *Pandani (Richea pandanifolia)*

121

PLATE 36   *New snow*

PLATE 38 *Rodway Range, Mount Field National Park*

Endemic flora

According to A. B. Costin (*Characteristics and Use of Australian High Country*) some 50% of Tasmania's mountain flora is endemic. These include shrubby conifers (*Pherosphera, Microcachrys, Diselma*) and the cushion plants which are considered to be of great scientific interest. In the high mountain regions Richeas are distinctive when in flower. The most common is said to be *Richea sprengelioides* whereas the most brilliant is *Richea scoparia* which often occurs in large areas flowering in glowing reds or orange-reds.

The endemic Tanglefoot (*Nothofagus gunnii*) intrigues botanists because it does not appear to be related to "other elements in the Australian flora". Thistle Y. Harris in *Alpine Plants of Australia* says that "some students think that the species migrated northwards from Antarctica along a continuous land mass with a cool moist climate which united the present northern continents with Antarctica." Another view is that this species with others had "their origin in North America and reached Australia along the western shore of the Pacific".

126

PLATE 39 *Flowers of Climbing Heath (Prionotes cerinthoides) in sub-alpine rainforest at*

Mount Anne

PLATE 40 *Huon Pines (Dacrydium franklinii) in the Truchanas Huon Pine Reserve, Denison River*

PLATE 41 *Christmas Bells (Blandfordia punicea)*

130

PLATE 42 *Deciduous Beech (Nothofagus gunnii) at Pine Valley, Lake St. Clair*

PLATE 43 *Hewardia (Isophysis tasmanica)*

PLATE 44   *Cushion plants at Pandani Shelf on Mount Anne with Mount Lot in background.*

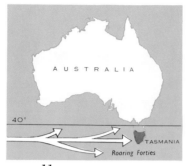

ILLUS. 11

LOCALITY PLAN SOUTH—WEST TASMANIA

ILLUS. 12

* The boundaries of the South-West National Park were recently re-defined, making it possible to show this on the map opposite in time for the third edition of this book.

Tasmania lies in the path of the "Roaring Forties", the latitudes that bear rain-laden winds that circle the southern oceans almost ceaselessly.

The South-West wilderness of the island is largely the result of this feature of its climate. Ten thousand miles of rolling sea, uninterrupted by any land mass, lie between Tasmania and South America. The west coast of Tasmania lies in wait to stem eastward moving ocean swells and storms.

The South-West coast has been carved and moulded into fantastic shapes of rock, bays and islands. Only two natural harbours offer any refuge.

Behind the coast range upon range of spectacular mountains rise sharply from the plains to intercept and subdue by degrees the great westerlies as they flow over the land to the sun-warmed areas of the east.

Tasmania's South-West is regarded by conservationists as one of the most important living assets in Australia, and is the sole surviving wilderness area of its kind in the world.

It is also highly vulnerable. Fire has already destroyed vegetation that cannot recover. It is threatened by mining and forestry operations. Many of its most superb features are included in the damming of rivers, and the flooding of lakes and valleys for hydro-electric development.

Only the nation can save this last great wilderness. *

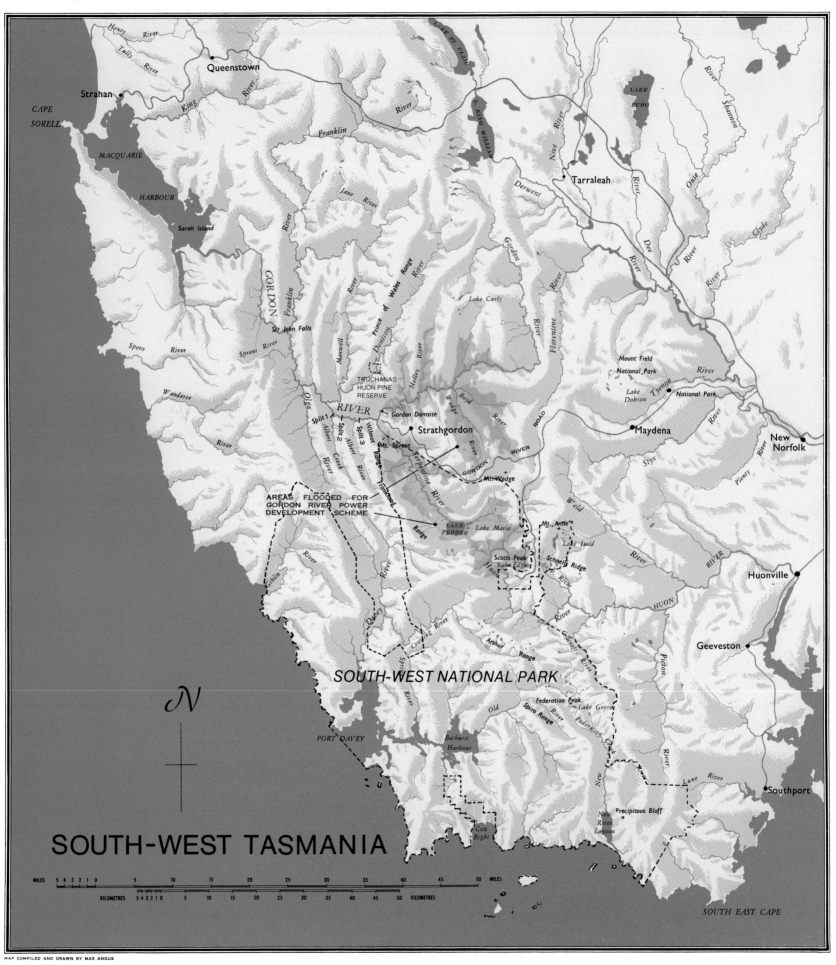

SOUTH-WEST TASMANIA

ILLUS. 13

MAP COMPILED AND DRAWN BY MAX ANGUS

Bibliography

1 Said to author by M. Truchanas.

2 Letter of B. Stasionis—11.1.73 Estate of M. Truchanas.

3 Said to author by E. Vaughan.

4 *The Mercury*, Hobart, 12.4.1928.

5 *ibid.*

6 O. Truchanas' diary (summary only) 1954. Estate of M. Truchanas.

7 *ibid.*

8 O. Truchanas' diary (2nd Gordon trip 1957-1958). Estate of M. Truchanas

9 *ibid.*

10 *ibid.*

11 *ibid.*

12 *ibid.*

13 *ibid.*

14 O. Truchanas' diary (summary only) 1954. Estate of M. Truchanas.

15 *The Mercury*, Hobart, 12.4.1928.

16 *ibid.*

17 *ibid.*

18 In notes written to author c. 1973, by M. Truchanas.

19 Private papers of O. Truchanas— 1967-71. Estate of M. Truchanas.

20 *ibid.*

21 Said to author by M. Truchanas

22 Letter of J. De Bavay. Estate of M. Truchanas.

23 *ibid.*

24 *ibid.*

25 *ibid.*

26 *The Mercury*, Hobart, 1965.

27 Letter of O. Truchanas to Australian Conservation Foundation, 10.11.68.

28 Private papers of O. Truchanas— 1967-71. Estate of M. Truchanas: letter dated 17.11.69.

29 *ibid.* 1.12.69.

30 *ibid* 1.12.69.

31 *ibid.* 5.2.70.

32 Letter of O. Truchanas to Australian Conservation Foundation, 22.2.70.

33 *Tasmanian Government Gazette*— 5.8.70.

34 From a tape of an A/V lecture by O. Truchanas.

35 O. Truchanas at Art Exhibition, Richmond, Tasmania, 19.11.71.

36 Private papers of O. Truchanas— 1967-71. Estate of M. Truchanas.

37 Said to author by R. D. Barnes— 7.1.72

38 Inspector T. E. Howard (Tasmania Police) in *Saturday Evening Mercury*, Jan. 1972.

Notes

CANOE (KAYAK): The photograph on page 14 is from a colour transparency made by Olegas Truchanas during his first Gordon River trip. It was given to Ralph Hope-Johnstone in 1958, and is one of the few to survive the fire of 1967.

GALAXIID FISHES: Two very rare fish inhabited vanished Lake Pedder. They were *G. parvus* and *G. pedderensis*. See A. P. Andrews in *The Lake Country of Tasmania*, Royal Society of Tasmania, 1972, p. 105.

HEWARDIA: The old name of *Hewardia tasmanica* is now replaced by *Isophysis tasmanica*. See N. T. Burbidge in *Dictionary of Australian Plant Genera*, Angus & Robertson, Sydney, 1963, p 150 (plate 43).

HORIZONTAL: *Anodopetalum biglandulosum* is endemic to Tasmania where it inhabits temperate rain forests. See W. M. Curtis in *Student's Flora of Tasmania*, 1956, pp 176-177 (p. 26-30).

LAKE PEDDER: Substantial information on the Lake Pedder issue is contained in the following *Newsletters* of the Australian Conservation Foundation:

Vol. 3, No. 3, June 1971
,, 4, ,, 1, Feb. 1972
,, 4, ,, 2, April ,,
,, 4, ,, 4, Sept. ,,
,, 4, ,, 5, Dec. ,,

Vol. 5, No. 1, Feb. 1973
,, 5, ,, 2, June ,,
,, 5, ,, 3, July ,,

Also, the State Library of Tasmania Index lists published information under the following categories:

Lake Pedder & National Park, 492 items.

Lake Pedder Action Committee, 36 items.

Lake Pedder Federal Enquiry, 107 items.

Also, *Pedder Papers* (Anatomy of a Decision) Australian Conservation Foundation, Melbourne, 1972; *The Future of Lake Pedder*, Report of Lake Pedder Committee of Enquiry, June 1973—Reprinted by Lake Pedder Action Committee

MACQUARIE HARBOUR CONVICTS: See *The Penal Settlements of Van Diemen's Land*, Thomas James Lempriere, Royal Society of Tasmania, 1954, pp. 45-51. (p. 18)

MOUNTAIN PLANT COMMUNITIES: See W. M. Curtis & J. Somerville (The Vegetation) in *Handbook of Tasmania*, Ed. L. Cerutty, Hobart, 1949, pp. 51-57 (see Cushion plants plate 44).

PORTRAIT. The portrait of O. Truchanas on p. 55 was taken a few days before his death, by Ralph Hope-Johnstone.

PRONUNCIATION OF NAME: English-speaking friends of Olegas Truchanas tended to stress the second last syllables of each word, and pronounced his name thus: Oh-*lay*-gus Tru-*har*-nas.

In Lithuanian it is pronounced thus:

ˈɒlægʌs ˈtruxʌnʌs

PUBLISHED ARTICLE: The Gordon Splits, Olegas Truchanas, *The Tasmanian Tramp*, Hobart, No. 20, Jan., 1972. pp. 67-71.

PUBLISHED LETTERS: (Signed O. Truchanas)

The Mercury, Hobart, 15.1.59
The Mercury, Hobart, 25.2.59
The Mercury, Hobart, 27.3.62

PUBLISHED SALON PRINTS: (of O. Truchanas) in the *Australian Photo-Review*, (a) Vol. 58, No. 7, July, 1951 —Forest Veteran (b) Vol. 59, No 2, Feb. 1952—Death Valley. (c) Vol. 59, No. 4, April 1952—Impregnable.

Note: "Death Valley" depicts Barn Bluff in the Cradle Mountain-Lake St. Clair National Park; "Forest Veteran" stands in the Mt. Wellington Reserve near Hobart; "Impregnable" depicts Nicoles Needle, Frenchman's Cap National Park; Untitled (p. 39) was photographed in Mt. Field National Park. All were printed by Olegas Truchanas. Untitled print No. 5 (p. 48) is from a negative found in his collection and printed by Frank Bolt. The subject is a tarn near Lake Picone, and Lot's Wife.

Index